BODOS CONVERSION TO MUSLIM

MUHAMMAD BIN BEPARI

Made with ♥ on the Notion Press Platform
www.notionpress.com

Contents

CHAPTER ONE

INTRODUCTION

The Bodo are a tribal people who live in northeast India. Most are Hindus but a small group converted to Islam during the Mughal period. Their primary occupations are agriculture, fishing and animal husbandry.

The main languages of the Bodo are Boro and Assamese. Christian resources are available in both languages.

CHAPTER TWO

WHERE ARE THEY LOCATED

The Muslims among the Bodo people live in Assam, a state in northeastern India. Some also live in Bangladesh.

CHAPTER THREE

WHAT ARE THEIR LIVES LIKE

Most of the Muslim Bodo live in villages in houses built of stone and wood. They grow rice, melons, vegetables, and yams. They will eat meat except for pork. Most families raise chickens and goats and may have a cow for milk. The Bodo make mats and articles from bamboo. Village elders decide legal cases and deal with outsiders. A Bodo man may have more than one wife if he can afford more. Sons inherit property with the eldest son becoming head of the family when the patriarch dies. Families arrange marriages within their group. Dancing and music play a big part of their important ceremonies such wedding, births and holidays.

CHAPTER FOUR

WHAT ARE THEIR BELIEFS

Though most of the Bodo people of India are part of their own ethnic religion blended with Hinduism, there is a small number that is Muslim. Like many South Asian Muslims, they are not very orthodox in their Islamic beliefs. They are loyal to the Islamic religious system, but on a daily basis, they look to the spirit world for help.

CHAPTER FIVE

BODOS CONVERSION TO ISLAM

Like Hinduisation, the Process of Islamisation was also taken place among the people of Bodo origin. The Process of Islamisation gained little importance in the writings of 19th century Indian historians. During this period the primary issue before the Indian intelligentsia was building of Indian Nationalism. At that time Indian writers were busy in the affairs of the reconstruction of Indian history and building of Indian Nationalism. Orthodox Hindu writers try to reconstruct Indian Nationalism based on the glories and prides of ancient Hindu culture and civilization. Orthodox Hindu intelligentsia blamed the Muslim rules for the downfall, misfortunes and miseries of Hindu civilization in India. Similarly the Muslims were also very much proud of their Muslim ascendancy in India and enthusiastic in tracing their relation with the Sultans and Islamic culture and civilization of the Asia minor. The real history of the autochthonous people remains beyond the purview of both the Hindu and Muslim scholars. Still, we don't have any history or records on which we can reconstruct the socio-cultural history the people of Eastern and North-eastern India.

Prior to the advent of the British people in India, the entire Bengal and Some parts of Assam came under the domination of Mugal Empire. Muslim period in Indian history is the vital period when lots of people from greater Bengal and Assam, had converted into Islam. But we have little information about the process in which conversion of mass people into Islam was taken place. The converted Muslims did not maintain any record about their proto-Islamic culture and civilization. It is similar to converted Hindus. Newly inducted Hindus, once they converted to Hinduism never look back to their pre-Hindu socio-cultural history and identity due to infamy of polluted and low-grade origin of their clan or lineage. In principle, Islam considers non-Muslim as Kafer. So, it is obviously undesirable on the part of newly inducted Muslims to identify themselves as the descendents of the Kafer and kept their proto-Islamic socio-cultural identity secret and rather, always try to trace their relation with the Islamic culture and civilization of the west. During the first half of the nineteenth century entire Bengal and Northeastern region was gone under the control of the British imperialism. During their regime, the British government in India collected information regarding

Indian societies, cultures, history, geography, ethnography, archaeology, economic institutions, political institution, religious institution, languages etc. of the contemporary Bengal and Assam. The objective was to understand the basic problems of the people of these areas for the purpose of planning, political decision and civil administration. This information collected by the British government reflects some important aspects of history and socio-cultural life of the people of ancient Bengal and Assam. It also reflects some important information regarding mass conversion of Mech or Bodos and other people of Bodo origin into Islam. On the basis of this information we may come into some important conclusion regarding the origin, migration, settlement, extension of the Bodo people and their language, culture and civilization in different parts of India in ancient time.

Tracing out the racial, ethnic or linguistic identity of the people of prehistoric India is a great challenge for the scholars from all disciplines. Thousands years of growth and development of Hindu civilization brought a number groups with distinct ethno-racial identity within the fold of Hindu Social structure. These distinct groups formed integral units of the structural and functional systems of Hindu social structure performing different types of social functions according to their fitness. These structural and functional units are known as *'jati'* or *'caste'*. Caste groups are functional units. It dose not represent any race, ethnic or linguistic group. Hindu social structure is a melting pot in which different groups of people with different culture; language, ethnic and race etc come into and melt in together to form distinct structural and functional units of Hindu society. To trace out the proto-Hindu socio-cultural identity from and within the existing Hindu social structure is quite difficult. Therefore, the efforts must be supported by the archaeological evidence, philological studies, ethnography, history of political, economic, religious institution, influence of nature on human biology and culture etc. Classical literature defined the eastern land, or the 'Prachya' as the abodes of Asura, Danava, Rakshasa, and Daityas etc. The terms Asura, Danava etc are also not sufficient to identify the culture, language and civilization of the pre-historic India. The information collected by the government official, historians, ethnographers, geologists, anthropologists, linguists, archaeologists, planner etc are much more reliable than any classical literature. On the basis these information we may try to define the areas inhabited by the people of Bodo origin and subsequently how Buddhism, Hinduism of different cults and Islam influenced them. Still, we do not have authentic source of information on Islamization as a process of conversion and assimilation. This would be a feeble effort for depicting a gloomy picture of conversion of the people of Bodo origin into

Islam.

The Census, conducted by the British Government during the last part of 19th century and first part of 20th century brought some vital statistics regarding the population on caste and race dimension. The fixation of race, caste etc. was very much influenced by the contemporary theory of Aryanism based on the principles of superiority and inferiority of culture, mental faculty, purity-impurity of blood, physical traits, like shape, size, height, texture and colour of the body etc. In the racial stratification, entire tribal and low caste and under developed communities were brought under non-Aryan race; and the ruling and high caste categories were brought under Aryan race. Modern researches based on genetic engineering, bio-technology accompanied with inter disciplinary approaches says that castes strata, higher and lower, pure and impure, dominant or dominated are not a racial categories, rather they are functionally arranged socio-cultural groups. Much has been discussed about race and reasons for biological variation and racial affiliation of the Bodos in the previous chapters. However the demographic information in the forms of vital statistics recorded in the Census reports are stated below for understanding the distribution of Bodo population in ancient time in Great Bengal.

Rajshahi was originally formed a part of the kingdom of *Pundra* or *Paundra Vardhana*, the country of the Pod or Bodos. During the rules of Sen dynasty, it was known as *Barendra Bhumi* (*Baro+Indra=Barendra*), the Land of the *Baro king*. Philological explanation of the term '*Barendra*' in Sanskrit language will read thus; *Baro + Indra: Baro* means twelve and *Indra* means kings, i.e., a *kingdom of twelve kings*. This type of reading is very much doubtful, because, there cannot be a kingdom with twelve kings. Further archaeology and history of this area tells us that, once the Kings of Varman, Pal, Sen dynasties who were by racially Boro origin, ruled this area. Therefore, the derivation of *Barendra* as the land or kingdom of Baro king is more scientific and rational than the *kingdom of twelve kings*. The term Baro is used as synonyms of the Baro (Twelve). This might be misinterpolation and misrepresentation by the of the 19th century scholars. Baro *bhuya*, *Baro thirtho*, *Barendra bhumi*, *Baro mahari*, *Barodawan*, *etc terms* undoubtedly comes within same category. According to the census of 1901, the number of Mohammedan population was-11,35,202 and constituted 77.6 % of the total population of the district. The number of Hindu population was 3,25,111 and constitutes 22.4% only. The census report says that majority of the Muslims were Sheikh and undoubtedly descendents of the Chandalas and the Koch. Still this people constitute major portion of the Hindu population.[1] Chandala is a generic term given to Non-Hindu people by the caste Hindus. They were called Chandalas because they did not follow the norms of Hindu religion. According to Dharmasatra of Manu, Chandlas are those who are ostracized due to their sinful activities and heinous crime from the caste Hindu society. Offsprings of the Pratiluma union are also identified as Chandala, according to Hindu dharma sastra. Chandalas of Bengal comes under the first category. Neither their ancestors committed any heinous crime nor they are descendent of the real Chandalas ostracized by the Caste Hindu society. They cannot be equated with the offspring of the ostracized members of the caste Hindu society as defined by dharmasastra. In earlier chapter it was shown that, Varman, Sen, Salstambha, and Pal kings themselves admitted that they were the descendents of Hirimba-Bhagadatta of Asura dynasty. Chandalas of Rajshahi were the subjects of Sen kings. From linguistic point of view also the people of the district are belonged to Koch-Rajbongshi.Because the dialect known as the Northern Bengali (Rajbongshi dialect) was the vernacular of the district.[2] There is maximum possibility of the Koch origin of the Chandalas of Rajshahi. Concept of Chandala stated in Hindu Sastra does not represent any race or ethnic people rather it represents an ostracized group of Hindus of Puranic times committing heinous crime and the descendent of illicit union of Brahmin women and Sudra male (protiluma union) and subsequently on whom the impure functions were assigned by the ruling and dominant castes. Once, the concept of Chandala exerts so much of influence on depressed caste people that, they prefer to be recognized themselves as the descendent of the illicit union of Brahmin mother and Sudra father rather than other wise.

Dinajpur is identified as *Matsyadesha*=(Land of the Fishes or fishermen) (Virat) of the epic age. In Bodo language, *di* means water *or river, na* means fish *and pur* means abode or place. Full meaning is *Land of the Fishing Cultivation or Land, abode of the fishes.* Subsequently Virata formed part of Barendra and then the kingdom of *Paudra-vardhana* with capital at Mahisthana. The term *Bordhan* or *Bordwan* (*Bwrdwanary*) is still popularly used to identfy the Bodo people living in greater Jalpaiguri area by the rest of the Bodo people. The ancestors of the *Bordhonary* or *Bodwanary* might have migrated from the areas ruled by the Vardhan kings. Structurally they speak pure Bodo language but their tune or phonetics of language is quite different from the Bodos of the other areas.

Once Dinajpur was constituted a part of the kingdom of Mahipal-I who was the descendent of Asura dynasty. Raja Ganesh from the line of Mahipal was the last Hindu King who converted into Islam. He seized the power of Bengal in 1404 and his dynasty occupied the throne until 1442.[3] Generally mass conversion took place along the conversion of the king into Islam. According to the Census of 1901, the total population of Dinajpur District was 15,67,080. The number of Mohammedans constituted 7,76,737 and the Hindus 7,26,429. The Rajbongshi dialect-speaking people constituted one third of the entire district and the Muslims were mainly derived from the same stock. This indicates that how the people of Koch-Bodo origin converted to Islam in a mass level.[4] Jalpaiguri was the land, which came under the jurisdiction of Kamatapur and Koch Behar. Earlier it was also part of Pal and Sen Kingdoms, the descendent of the Asuras. Subsequently Biswa Singh formed Koch kingdom. According to the Census of 1901, the total population of Jalpaiguri district was 787,380. Hindu population constituted 5,34,625(68%) and Mahammedan-2,28,487(29%). The Muslim populations primarily constituted of Sheikh and Nasyas, and are most part, converted from the neighboring Koch and Mech races. The Muslims, then, had retained many beliefs and superstition derived from their ancestors, and lived on good terms side by side with Rajbongshis and more than three fifth of the Hindu populations constituted of the Rajbongshis.[5] 77% of the total population spoke Rongpuri or Rajbongshi dialect. This population consisted of both Hindus and Muslims who might have common ancestor in the past.[6] Affiliation to Rajbongshi language and ethnicity clearly indicates that converted Muslims of Jalpaiguri district was ethnologically belonged to Koch-Bodo group.

Malda district was a part of Pundra or Paundra Vardhana of the Puranic time. Subsequently became the part Barendra Bhumi and ruled by Sen dynasty. From the early part of 12th century, this area had gone under the occupation of the Mohammedans. According to Census of 1901;the total population of Malda district was 8,844,030. Hindu population constituted 50% and Muslim population constituted of 48% of the total population. Almost all the Muslims were Sheikh, they probably for the most part of descended from the Rajbongshis or Koch who form the prevailing race of North Bengal to the east of Mahnanda and who constituted the most numerous Hindu caste in the district.[7] Mahananda was the linguistic boundary. Northern dialect (Rajbongshi dialect) was spoken by both Muslims and Hindu in the eastern parts of the District.

Rongpur was just adjacent to Koch Behar and Goal Para and Garo hills districts. In ancient time Rongpur formed the western outpost of ancient Hindu Kingdom of Kamrupa. According to local tradition, Rongpur was the abode of pleasure of Raja Bhagadatta. *Rong* means pleasure and *pur* means town or habitat. This area constituted a part of the kingdom of the Pal, Sen, Koch dynasty and known as Kamatapur and Koch Bihar. In 1661, the entire Rongpur was gone to the occupation of the Mughal rulers. Nearly two third of the Hindu population were Rajbongshis.Many Vaisnavas were recruited from this category of people. The total number of Mohammedan population was-13,71,430(64%) and the Hindus 7,76,6469 (36%). Almost all the Muslim population (92%) was sheikh and (8%) was Nasyas. Of the Musalmans are probably descendents of converts from the aboriginal Hindu caste. "The Aryan caste is very poorly represented".[8] The term 'aboriginal Hindu caste' is to be examined carefully from archaeological, historical and linguistic, anthropological, sociological perspectives and also evolutionary perspectives of social and biological dynamics. Historically Rongpur was the abode of King Bhagadatta. In the epic he had been stated as the king of Kiratas and referred as *Mleccha-adhipati*. In the classical literature *Pracchya* was referred as the land of non-Aryan. After Bhagadatta, successively Barman, Sen, Pal, and Salstabha, Koch dynasty ruled this area upto Orissa and Kanauj and claimed themselves as the descendents of Hiramba-Bhagadatta. The language spoken in this area is known as Rongpuri or Rajbongshi language.[9] Hence the term 'aboriginal Hindu caste strongly suggested to the Koch-Bodo people who are racially belonged to Kirat-Bodo and who adopted Hinduism much earlier. Identifying them with Dravir is historically fallacious. Because all the rulers stated above were the descendents of Naraka-Bhagadatta and Heramba dynasty. Caste as a system of structural-functional divisions had attained full features among the people of Rongpur long before the arrival of Islam there. In the process of the formation of Hindu social structure, socio-economically and politically weaker sections of the society always occupy lower ranks in the caste hierarchy. On contrary, the wealthy and men of power occupied higher status on the other hand. Achievement of high status is conditioned by the possession of wealth, power, and mastery over skill and knowledge on particular field like religion, art, craft, medicine etc. Koch-Rajbonshis of North Bengal adopted Hinduism much later than the Rajbongshis of Rongpur, Sylhet, and Moimonsigh etc. Hence there is little doubt on the Rajbongshi origin of Mahmaddens of Rongpur.When Raja Biswa Singh was initiated into throne after conversion to Hinduism he directly achieved the status of Kshatriyahood and mass of the common people were put down to low grade Sudra status. Common people were disgusted with their low position in the society. Being disgusted by their degraded social position they converted into Islam. Low grade Sudra due to poverty and economic hardship develop different type biological and socio-economic features a bit different from the high caste people though they had been originally descendents of the same ancestor.

In ancient time Bogra was a part of Kamrupa and subsequently of Pundra and Barendra. Bogra also came under the occupation of Mohammedans. While stating the demographic position of the Bogra district it was recorded that the total population was-8,54,533. Muslims constituted 6,99,185(82%) and Hindu constituted-1,54,131(18%) only according to the census of 1901.Mahammedans were mostly and probably descendents of the converts from the Koch Rajbongshis of North Bengal. Rajbongshis still constituted major part of Hindu population. In fact conversion to Islam was taken place on a large scale seems to be shown by the number of villages which bear Hindu names but no Hindu habitations.[10] Muslim Sultans and Governors were the forerunners of Islam religion. They took vital roles in spreading and conversion to Islam religion everywhere. They were the agents of the extension of Islam among the non-Islam particularly the depressed castes and tribes.

According to the Census of 1901, the total number of Mohammedan population in Pabna district was-16, 50,000 and Hindu-9,88,000. Almost all the Muslims population was Shaikh (15,56,000) and most of who were undoubtedly the descendents of converted lower Hindu caste probably the remnances of the aboriginal race. Most probably they were belonged to Koch-Mech stock because lower caste people were commonly derived from Koches and Meches especially in eastern and northern Bengal. Ballan Sen the most famous Hindu ruler of Sen dynasty of.Bengal held his court here in Pabna, and at the earliest date it was under the rule of Adisur who was identified with the founder of Sen dynasty. 'Cunningham conjectured that the name of Pabna is derived from Pundra whose capital was at Mahasthan.' The vernacular of the district is known as Northern Bengali or Rajbongshi dialect, the language of the Koch-Rajbongshi. Hence, Pabna is historically and linguistically belonged to Koch-Rajbongshi.

In ancient time Dacca was a part of the Kingdom of Sen. and Pal dynasty. At an earlier date it was under the rule of Adisur, most probably the ancestor of Narka-Bhagadatta who has been identified with the founder of Sen dynasty.[11] In ancient time the people of non-Aryan origin, most probably of Kirata-Asura, predominantly inhabited this area. After 1199 the Muslim rulers consecutively ruled this area until 1757.According to the census of

1901 the Mohammedan population numbered 1,650'000 more than three fifth of the total population. Hindu constituted only 988,000, only 37% of the total population. The Majority of the Muslims are Shaikhs most of whom are doubtlessly the descendent of converts from Chandalas and Koches. (Ibid, 300). Refined Bengali is the Vernacular language of the district. The language of the south is more refined and formal than the north. It might be due to earlier contact of the south with western culture, civilization, and education etc. The movement of the origin and development of Modern Bengali language and culture started from south, i., e., Calcutta, Dhaka etc. That might be the reason why Chandalas of Bengal became much advance in comparison to the people of north and also other backward castes from other parts of India. Structurally and functionally rigid caste groups are evident in South Bengal. Their sense of self-respect and identity movement was the consequence of contact with the western civilization. Chandala name was coined by the by the high Caste Hindu people to show their superiority over them. The nineteenth century colonial explanation for the geographical anchorage of these people was their tribal origin, as territoriality was believed a salient feature of the tribes. Ronel Inden, in his work 'Imagining India' says the Namasudras (Chandalas) as 'Non-Aryan autochthonous people of the land.' The theory certainly appears to have been derived from the late nineteenth century racial ethnology of the colonial officials like Herbert Risely, who divided the Indian population into two racial types, as the Aryan and Dravidian and held that a tribe was development out of race, while a caste was a development out of tribe." In Risely's typology, the Namasudras (Chandalas) appeared as tribal, who had gradually embraced Hinduism, accepted the Hindu social organization and thus had hardened into caste.[12] James Wise also had observed in purely racialist tone that the Chandalas were a Dravidian tribe... But they did not put any scientific reason in favour of their remarks. While stratifying the people of Bengal and other place, they took under consideration the eighteenth century racial theories in which solely biological traits were taken as the dimensions for racial stratification. They did not consider the influence geographical condition on biological adaptation and variation, long time of habitation in the area, Political history, extension and development of Indo-Aryan language in this area, archaeological evidences etc. Archaeological evidence say that entire Bengal since pre-historic time was ruled by the kings of Kirata Asura Origin from beginning Varman dynasty to Koch Kings. In the Mahabharata also it was clearly stated that the land ruled by Narka was inhabited primarily by the Kiratas. Bhagadatta was also referred as the King of Mleccha, 'mlecchadhipati'. The founder of Varman dynasty, Pushya Varman' was closely related to Salstambha line. In the Borgaon Coperplate Grant [13] of Ratnapala, Salstambha was identified as Mlecha Overlord. On the basis of the Borgaon Coperplate Dr. S.K. Chatterjee firmly says that Salstambha were Bodo (Mech) Chief sanskritized as Mletccha.[14] Madhya Roy, the first king of Sen dynasty the founders Kamotapur kingdom are undoubtedly Koch-Mech origin. According to Bucchanon, Nilodhwaj of Kamatapur was of Asura origin. Common subject Rajbongshis considered him as the member of their race.[15] The Pal kings claimed themselves to the origin of Bhagadatta dynasty.

Mymensingh district once formed a part of ancient Kamrupa or Pragjyotishpura and ruled by great Kirata King Bhagadatta. His Kingdom was extended up to sea and erected his capital in Madhupur. The site of the remnances of his palace is in Madhupur Jungle at place known *Baro Thirtha*.[16] The kings and dynasties of Kirata-Asura origin consecutively ruled this area. It was a part of the Kingdom of Barman, Sen, Pal, Salstambha and Koch dynasty. After 1199 Eastern Bengal including Mymensingh gradually gone under the occupation of the Mohammedans. According to the census of 1901, total population of Mymensingh district was 3,915,068. Muslims constituted 2,795,548 and Hindus-1, 088,857 and animist 28,958. Majority of the Muslims are the descendents of the aboriginal races whose representatives are still numerous in the district, namely Chandala, Koch, and Hazong etc. Chandalas and Koibartas are the people living in swampy and low lying area dealing basically with fishing culture. The environment they live shapes the structure and pattern of their socio-economic and cultural life. Chandals and Kaivarta represent more or less similar type of cultural groups possessing pattern of egalitarian society without caste stratification within them. Extension of Indo-Aryan language and culture on the people of eastern Bengal was perhaps older than the north. Some people of Garo origin like, Hadzong (High landers), Hadis (people living in swampy area), Dulas (people living in low lying area all of three are purely Bodo terms) speaks corrupt Bengali Language.[17] Hinduisation as a process of absorption of tribes and non-Hindus supports the racial origin of the Chandala, Kaibarta and many caste Hindu groups to be Koch-Bodo-Garo etc origin. Political history of Bengal also says that this area once was entirely inhabited by the people of Kirata-Asura origin.

In ancient time Faridpur district came under the jurisdiction of Banga what is called by Hiuen Tsang as Samatata. The people of Chandala origin primarily inhabited this area. During the time of Jahangir, many tribal chiefs known as *Bara Bhuya* ruled this country. Chand Rai, Kedar Rai, Sitaram Rai are the examples.[18] Total population in 1901 was 1,937,646. 62% of the population is Muslim .The vast majority of the Muslim people are Shaikhs the descendent of Converted Chandalas who are still constituted majority of the Hindu population. Structurally and functionally well-shaped caste groups are found in this area. Census reports say that, Muslims Shaikhs from most parts of Bengal were traced their origin with Koch Rajbongshi.

CHAPTER SIX

REASONS FOR THE BODOS CONVERSION TO MUSLIM

The motto of the Muslim invasion of India was not only to establish their rule but also to spread Islam in the areas under their occupation. War as a part of Holy Spirit for the protection and propagation of Islam became a tradition for Muslim warriors, which was developed by the Muslims of the Asia miners during the Holly war that was taken in Palestine. That tradition and spirit was maintained by all Muslim warriors in all wars, particularly in every war against the non-Muslim country. Extension of Islam was also a part of extension of empire. It is only because of the patrons of the Sultans, the ideals of Islam extended through out Indian subcontinent. Indeed this was not a sole reason for spreading of Islam in Eastern and North-eastern India. Prior to the arrival of Islam the great Buddhism swept this area during the days of Bhaskarman. Bengal was the way through which Buddhism extended to East Asia. Archaeological remains found in different place in Bengal and the Charya padas, early Indian written literature found in Bengal also supported this contention. After Buddhism wave of Hinduism came which swept the entire Eastern and Northeastern India. It constituted as the process of social transformation until Muslim arrived in Bengal in the year 1199.

Social history written by different scholars suggests that caste system was already been found to exist in ancient Bengal in which Chandala, Asuras, Koches and other backward people occupied humiliating status in the society. Their socio-religious freedom and upward mobility in the society was restricted by number of stringents such as idea of purity-pollution, superior-inferior, possession of wealth, political and economic power etc. The entire designed was guided by the motives of the dominants, for domination over the others. People clearly understood it. But were quite help less and could do nothing to change their lots. And viable alternative remained before them was the Islam which was more liberal and far less discriminated in ideal and action than Hinduism. The principles of Islam, "Equality and brotherhood among men" as against the caste principles of Hinduism, "inequality, untouchability, discrimination, exploitation and suppression " people rationally attracted toward Islam and converted to it. Koch, Mech, Garo, Kachari, Rabha, Hazong etc. ....of ancient Kamrup, Koch Bihar and Kamatapur being denied honorable status in the society and instead of holding, *antyaja* or *polluted* status they preferred to accept Islam and converted to Islam.[19] High caste Hindu scholars hardly agree to this *conversion theory based on social disparity, suppression and exploitation.*. But there here is no doubt on the validity of this theory.

G.A.Grierson in his linguistic study in Rongpur and Dinajpur area found some Islamic element in Rajbongshi song and he was confirmed that some Rajbongshis converted into Islam.[20] In Dinajpur, Rongpur and Bagura converted Muslims are divided into Halia Keot and Jalia Keot.Halia Keots are agriculturists and Jalias are fisheris. Differences are found in socio-cultural life of the general Muslim and the Keot Muslims.[21] They had been pure Rajbongshis. Now these Muslim do not like to identify themselves as Rajbongshi.The studies carried by Fakkarujamman Choudhury proved this fact as ...[22] Because of the untouchability, nearly half of the lower caste population of Bengal converted to Islam during the period of Muslim ascendancy in Bengal.[23] Conversion theory is supported by the study of some modern social scientists.[24] Richard Easton, says, the spread of Islam in east Bengal need not be looked upon in terms of 'conversion'. Bengal being out side the core area of Brahmanical civilization, the rigorous of the caste system were much less oppressive here and therefore the social emancipation theory cannot help us understand the process. His view is partially true. As the frontier of the cultivation of the land extended in eastern Bengal between the sixteenth and the eighteenth centuries, Islam also spread as an ideology of civilization, as a religion of the plough' bringing local people gradually into its fold. This Islamization did not take place at one stroke., but as a gradual process, slowly absorbing the colonizers of the land, who were not yet touched or just slightly touched by Hinduism.[25]

Categories of caste group stated by Hitesh Ranjan Syanal, Partho Chttopadhyay etc might have been existed only in a Feudal agricultural society. Monarchy or Feudal political entity can be sustained only on agricultural economy. Sekhar Bondopadhyay supported the view of Richard Eaton and says that, the creation of Muslim peasantry was not the result of any large-scale conversion' of the Chandala, but gradual incorporation of the people living at the periphery of Brahmanical civilization. But it is seen that, the process of Islamization was taken place in different ways and conditioned by different factors.

The Hinduization of the frontier people as compare with the settled agricultural society in the west, took place rather at late stage, when the caste system had already assumed its fully developed shape and the outsider were being admitted only at the bottom of the social structure.[26] Still some of the non-Hindu groups denied free access in the caste Hindu society till the early decades of the twentieth century.[27] One of the earliest influences of Islam leading to conversion was that its egalitarian social philosophy had allured many Non-Islam into its fold. Mohammedanism in India are almost always such by birth and inheritance of many generations since the Mohammedan conquest. Through the era of Mugol Empire the leading persons of many parts of India were Mohammedans. They were caste group in the sense of being a religious group by themselves.

In 1417 AD, Danujmordan of Konch dynasty initiated Hindu kingdom in North Bengal. His son Mohendra Dev succeeded him. One of the sons of Mohendra Dev converted into Islam and adopted the Muslim and changed his name to Jalaluddin.[28] Perhaps he was influenced much by the egalitarian principle of the Islam contrary to the principles of social disparity and exploitation of caste Hindu society.

"In the middle part of the 18th century, Hazrot Abul Kasim Khorasani was born. He was enlightened by the principles of Islam and came India to advocate the massage of Allah among the people of India and subsequently came to lower Assam and passed away in 1896. His tomb is still in existence exposing on the hillock situated in the heart of Goalpara town. His handsome physical built and attractive personality attracted the common people of the area. More than twenty-five villages belonging to Rabha Community accepted Islam from this great saint. The people of these villages still consider themselves as the descendents the disciples of Khorasani.[29] In the middle part of the 19th century the great Sufi saint Hazrot Abul Kasim came to India to spread the massage of Islam. Later he migrated to lower Assam and stationed at South Goalpara. His handsome physical built and humbled and attractive personality attracted the people of the area. More than twenty-five villages belonging to Rabha community converted to Islam initiated by this great saint Hazrot Khorasani. The villagers of this vast area still consider them as the disciple of this great saint and claimed as the descendents of the Rabhas.The tomb of this great saint is still in appearance on the hillock.

It is severely alleged that Islamisation is extended through sword. But, the available records in Indian history say that, no Muslim invader invaded India with an objective of evangelizing people to Islam. Their primary objective was political, extention of kingdom, accumulation of wealth and property etc. They invaded India sometimes for extension of kingdom and sometime for establishment of new kingdom in India. Again sometime the invasion was made purely on the purpose of looting wealth and riches of India.

Stating the reason for Islamisation of the lower section of people in Bangladesh, Prof. Ismail Husain quoted Rabindra Nath Thakur as, "We know India as the land of *bhodrolok* (civilian), the number of Muslim converts in Bengal has gone up in increasing primarily for one reason, i., e., the Hindu gentlemen did not keep them embraced by heart." [30] The idea of purity and pollution, untouchability, high and low are the principles of caste Hindu society. Low caste or tribal people became the subject of social, economic, political, religious exploitation. The exploited section of people took the advent of Islam as an opportunity to expose their subaltern feeling against the years long suppression of the dominant caste. To escape from exploitation of the dominant caste they convert into Islam.

Islamization was not confined only to depressed sections of the society. The elite sections of the society were also converted into Islam on political and economic ground. Ali Mech the Bodo Chief of Alipur converted into Islam along with his Bodo subjects. The case of Jalaluddin is already stated. Many of the descendents of Barman, Pal, Sen, Kamata, Salastambha rulers and their subjects might have converted to Islam. There is an indication in the *Chaitanya Bhagabat* that even the Brahmins, the guardians of Hindu religion, were also converted into Islam for economic or political gain. In Chaitanya Bhagabat it is said-

"Hindu kule keho jeno hoiya Brahman,
Aponei giya hoi icchai jobon.
Hindu ba kikore tare, jar jei kormo,
Apone je moilo tare mariya ki dhormo" [31]

During the reign of Konch king Lakshmansen of Sen dynasty, of Komatapur, his minister Holayudh Mishra, wrote a biography, "Sheikh Subhodoy" on the life of Sheikh Jalaluddin. In this biography it is stated that, impressed by the ideals of Islam the Jallaluddin and many Tantricists of Bengal converted to Islam.[32] Koch king Viswa Singha, after initiation to Hinduism created a Rajbonshi genealogy for him tracing his origin to God Siva. Along with him large number of his subjects converted into Hinduism. But common converts were granted lower position in the social hierarchy. Being disgusted with there low status many subjects converted to Islam.

" According to one description, being failed to defeat the Komota king of Sen dynasty by sword, the Nabab of Gaur maintained peaceful religious methods of friendship and brotherhood. Nilambor, the son of Kamota king,

Chakradhar married a beautiful daughter of the Nabab of Gour.[33] On the basis of the foregoing discussion we may attribute the following factors as the reason for mass Islamisation of the people of Bodo-Koch and low caste origin up to the coming of British people in India: -

1. Islamisation as a way to escape from caste inequality and exploitation.
2. Islamisation for social security, liberty, equality, brotherhood, humanism and freedom.
3. For gaining Political and economic favour from the Muslim rulers.
4. Influence of Suphibad with the principles of liberty, egalitarianism, humanism.
5. Atrocities made by the Kings, Jaminders and Brahmins.
6. Due to ignorance and superstition common people became the easy target of Islamisation.

CHAPTER SEVEN

ALI MECH

Ali Mech was a tribal chief in the 13th century CE, in the region of present-day Assam belonging to the Mech people. He is said to have helped Bakhtiyar Khalji duing his Tibet campaign and converted to Islam under his influence.

Ali Mech	
Born	13th century Kamatapur Kingdom
Occupation	Tribal chief
Era	early 13th century
Known for	Tibet campaign

Biography

Ali Mech is considered the first Muslim convert in Assam.[1][2] In the wake of Ali Mech's conversion to Islam, some Mech and Koch tribes also adopted the faith.[3][4] The modern descendants of these converts are the Deshi people.[3]

As a tribal chief in the foothills of Kamrup,[5] he aided Bakhtiyar Khilji in his failed invasion of Tibet in 1206 by acting as a guide.[6]

E. A. Gait mentions that he guided Bakhtyar Khalji march northwards along the right bank of the Karatoya river (present-day Bangladesh) for ten days, through a country inhabited by the Koch, Mech and Tharu (Terai) tribes.

Ali Mech supposedly bears a Muslim first name because he fond of Islam and embraced it. Soon hundreds of Mech inhabitants converted to Islam due to growing oppression in the hands of Hindu lords and its caste, customs and traditions and as most of them were considered to be Yavanas or polluted outsiders by the Aryan hindus.[7][8]

CHAPTER EIGHT

CONCLUSION

Conclusion: - Till the establishment of British rule in India religion was never a factor of community sentiment or communalism. The electoral politics based on caste, community, religion, tribe etc. sowed the seeds of communalism. The sense of communalism may be eliminated by the application of rational scientific education replacing worldview based on religious belief, by the worldview based on science and rationality. Poverty, diseases, miseries, illiteracy, ignorance are the basic human problems in which the roots of communalism, regionalism, extremism, antinationalism etc rest in. Promotion and development of economic conditions of the people of the country will help in the elimination of anti human sentiments amongst the different sections of people.

9 798889 865841

Printed by Libri Plureos GmbH in Hamburg,
Germany